FIRST AID SAFETY

by Emma Bassier

Cody Koala

An Imprint of Pop!
popbooksonline.com

abdobooks.com
Published by Pop!, a division of ABDO, PO Box 398166, Minneapolis, Minnesota 55439. Copyright © 2021 by POP, LLC. International copyrights reserved in all countries. No part of this book may be reproduced in any form without written permission from the publisher. Pop!™ is a trademark and logo of POP, LLC.

Printed in the United States of America, North Mankato, Minnesota

052020
092020

THIS BOOK CONTAINS RECYCLED MATERIALS

Cover Photo: Shutterstock Images (background, scratch)
Interior Photos: Shutterstock Images, 1 (background), 1 (scratch), 5 (top), 5 (bottom left), 5 (bottom right), 6, 9, 10 (top right), 10 (bottom right); iStockphoto, 10 (top left), 10 (bottom left), 13, 15 (top), 15 (bottom left), 15 (bottom right), 16, 19, 20

Editor: Connor Stratton
Series Designer: Christine Ha

Library of Congress Control Number: 2019955002
Publisher's Cataloging-in-Publication Data
Names: Bassier, Emma, author.
Title: First aid safety / by Emma Bassier
Description: Minneapolis, Minnesota : POP!, 2021 | Series: Safety for kids | Includes online resources and index
Identifiers: ISBN 9781532167546 (lib. bdg.) | ISBN 9781532168642 (ebook)
Subjects: LCSH: First aid in illness and injury--Juvenile literature. | Health education--Juvenile literature. | Safety education--Juvenile literature. | Accidents--Prevention--Juvenile literature.
Classification: DDC 614.88--dc23

Hello! My name is

Cody Koala

Pop open this book and you'll find QR codes like this one, loaded with information, so you can learn even more!

Scan this code* and others like it while you read, or visit the website below to make this book pop.

popbooksonline.com/first-aid-safety

*Scanning QR codes requires a web-enabled smart device with a QR code reader app and a camera.

Table of Contents

Quick Help

Liam falls on the sidewalk. He scrapes his knee. He calls to his mom for help. She puts a bandage on his knee. When someone gets hurt, first aid can help.

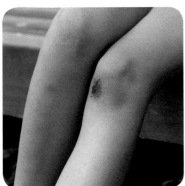

Watch a video here!

First aid is **medical** help that happens right after an **accident** or injury occurs. People can give first aid in many ways. They often use first aid kits. These kits have items such as bandages and tape. Some have medicine too.

Chapter 2

Treating a Cut

People bleed when they get cut. First, clean the cut. Wipe it gently. Use water to wash out bits of dirt or rock.

Complete an activity here!

Caring for a Cut

1. Wipe the cut gently.

2. Clean the area with water.

3. Put ointment on the cut.

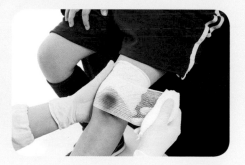

4. Cover the cut with a bandage.

Clean the area around the cut with soap. Then, put ointment on the cut. Ointment is a thick cream. It helps the cut heal. Next, choose a bandage to put on the wound.

Adhesive bandages

can cover small cuts.

But some cuts are too big

or deep. These cuts need

larger bandages.

> Sometimes doctors close big or deep cuts with stitches. They use special thread to sew the cuts closed.

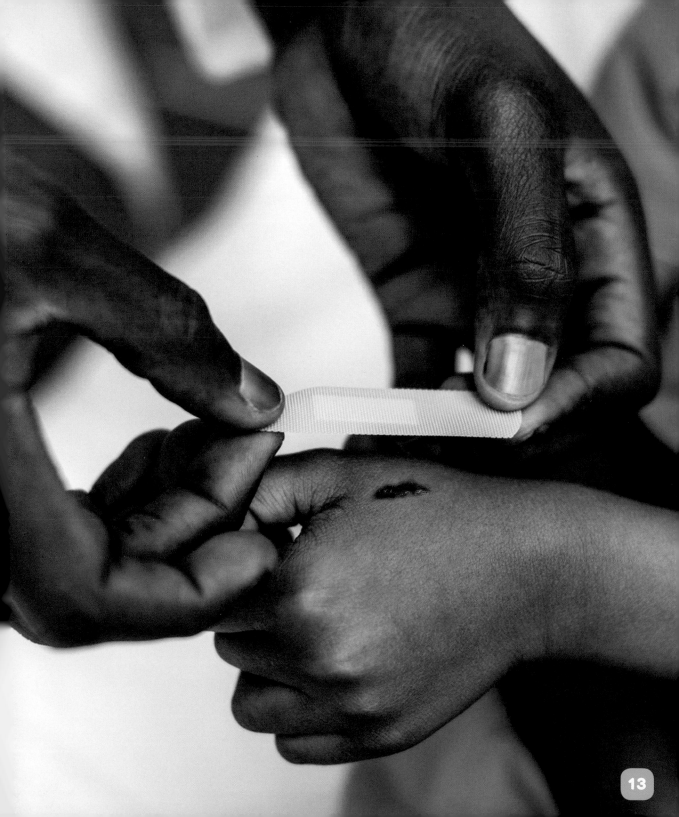

Chapter 3

Bumps and Bruises

Sometimes people become hurt, but they don't bleed. When people fall or get hit, they can get **bruises**. People can also twist their ankles while running.

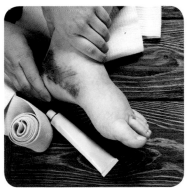

Learn more here!

Injuries to **joints** often swell. They puff up and turn red. You can use ice to help these injuries hurt less. Ice makes the area cold. The cold helps get rid of pain.

Chapter 4

Bigger Injuries

Sometimes people get seriously hurt. Broken bones and **fainting** are types of serious problems. So is bleeding that doesn't stop.

Learn more here!

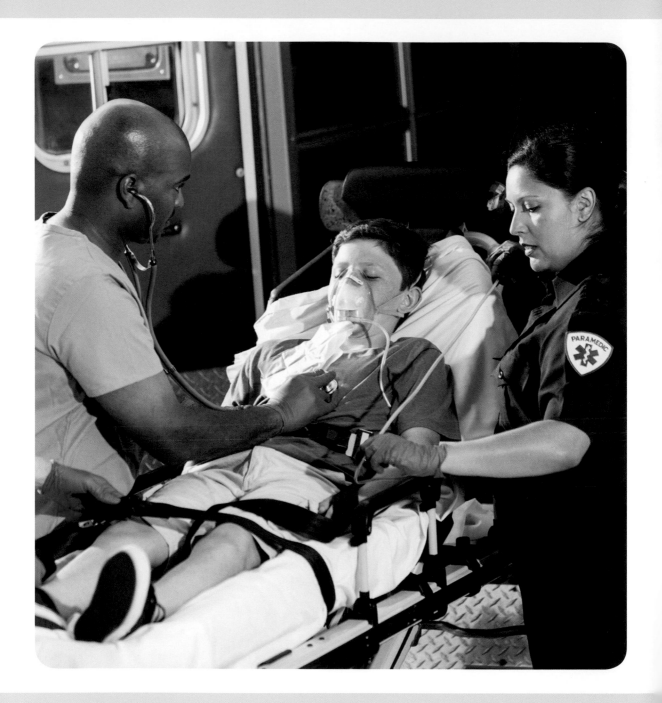

For serious injuries, some people may need more help than first aid. These people should go to the hospital. In an **emergency**, call 9-1-1. A team of **medical** workers will come quickly to help.

An ambulance is a vehicle that rushes people to the hospital.

Making Connections

Text-to-Self

Have you ever gotten a cut or bruise? What did you do to help it heal?

Text-to-Text

Have you read other books about safety tips? How were those safety tips similar to or different from the tips described in this book?

Text-to-World

First aid is a kind of medical help. Can you think of people or groups that help care for someone who is sick or injured?

Glossary

accident – something that is not planned and often harmful.

adhesive bandage – a small bandage that sticks to the skin to cover a wound.

bruise – a mark on the skin from an injury.

emergency – when something unsafe happens and calls for quick action.

faint – to fall down because the brain is not getting enough blood.

joint – a place in the body where two bones meet.

medical – having to do with doctors or medicine.

Index

Online Resources

popbooksonline.com

Thanks for reading this Cody Koala book!

Scan this code* and others like it in this book, or visit the website below to make this book pop!

popbooksonline.com/first-aid-safety

*Scanning QR codes requires a web-enabled smart device with a QR code reader app and a camera.